Introduction

As parents and educators, we recognize the pivotal role mathematics plays in shaping a child's academic journey and future success. Yet, the path to mathematical proficiency can often seem daunting, fraught with challenges and complexities. That's where the transformative power of MathFlare Workbooks shine through, illuminating the way forward with clarity, precision, and purpose.

Introducing MathFlare Workbooks – a beacon of guidance, a testament to excellence, and a catalyst for achievement. Crafted with meticulous care and expertise, MathFlare Workbooks stand as paragons of educational excellence, designed to nurture young minds, ignite a passion for learning, and develop a deep-rooted understanding of mathematical concepts.

Picture this: your child eagerly delves into the pages of Mathflare Workbook, greeted by a step-by-step guide illuminated with vivid examples that demystify complex mathematical concepts. With each turn of the page, they embark on a journey of discovery, encountering thoughtfully curated practice questions that reinforce learning and hone problem-solving skills. And when they unveil the answers to those very questions, a sense of accomplishment blossoms within them – a tangible reward for their hard work and dedication.

But MathFlare Workbooks are more than just tools for learning; they are pathways to comprehension, fostering a deep-seated understanding of mathematical concepts through a sequential, logical flow. From fundamental principles to advanced problem-solving strategies, every chapter builds upon the last, ensuring a robust foundation upon which future knowledge can be constructed.

As parents, we yearn for nothing more than to see our children thrive, to witness the spark of inspiration ignited within them as they conquer academic challenges with confidence and poise. MathFlare Workbooks serve as partners in this noble endeavor, offering not just practice questions, but the keys to unlocking a world of opportunity.

And for teachers, MathFlare Workbooks stand as invaluable allies in the quest to cultivate mathematical proficiency in the classroom. With answers readily available, instructors can focus on guiding and nurturing their students, confident in the knowledge that MathFlare Workbooks provide a solid framework upon which to build.

In the pages of MathFlare Workbooks, we find not just the promise of academic excellence, but the seeds of a brighter tomorrow. So let us embrace the power of mathematics, let us champion the journey of learning, and let us pave the way for a generation of young minds poised to shape the world. With MathFlare Workbooks as our guide, the possibilities are infinite, and the future, bright.

Table of Contents

MathFlare
Grade 2
MATH WORKBOOK
Step by Step Guide and Essential Practice with Answers
Addition Subtraction
Multiplication
Place Value and Expanded Notations
Geometry
MathFlare Publishing

MathFlare
Grade 2-3
MATH WORKBOOK
Step by Step Guide and Essential Practice with Answers
Addition Subtraction
Multiplication and Division
Place Value and Expanded Notations
Geometry
MathFlare Publishing

MathFlare
Grade 3
MATH WORKBOOK
Step by Step Guide and Essential Practice with Answers
Multiplication and Division
Decimals
Place Value and Expanded Notations
Fractions and Geometry
MathFlare Publishing

MathFlare
Grade 1
MATH WORKBOOK
Step by Step Guide and Essential Practice with Answers
Counting and Numbers
Addition and Subtraction
Place Value and Expanded Notations
Understanding Time
MathFlare Publishing

MathFlare
Grade 1-2
MATH WORKBOOK
Step by Step Guide and Essential Practice with Answers
Counting and Numbers
Addition and Subtraction
Place Value and Expanded Notations
Understanding Time
MathFlare Publishing

MathFlare
Grade 3-4
MATH WORKBOOK
Step by Step Guide and Essential Practice with Answers
Addition Subtraction
Multiplication Division
Place Value and Expanded Notations
Fractions and Geometry
MathFlare Publishing

MathFlare
Grade 4
MATH WORKBOOK
Step by Step Guide and Essential Practice with Answers
Addition Subtraction
Multiplication Division
Place Value and Expanded Notations
Fractions and Geometry
MathFlare Publishing

MathFlare
Grade 4-5
MATH WORKBOOK
Step by Step Guide and Essential Practice with Answers
Multiplication Division
Place Value and Expanded Notations
Fractions and Geometry
Unit Conversion
MathFlare Publishing

MathFlare
MATH WORKBOOK
5
Step by Step Guide and Essential Practice with Answers
Multiplication Division
Place Value and Expanded Notations
Fractions and Geometry
Unit Conversion
MathFlare Publishing

MathFlare
MATH WORKBOOK
5-6
Step by Step Guide and Essential Practice with Answers
Multiplication Division
Place Value and Expanded Notations
Fractions and Geometry
Units and Statistics
MathFlare Publishing

MathFlare
MATH WORKBOOK
6
Step by Step Guide and Essential Practice with Answers
Integers and Statistics
Arithmetic and Pre-Algebra
Fractions and Geometry
Ratio and Percentage

MathFlare
MATH WORKBOOK
6-7
Step by Step Guide and Essential Practice with Answers
Arithmetic and Pre-Algebra
Ratio, Percent Proportion
Geometry
Statistics
MathFlare Publishing

MathFlare
MATH WORKBOOK
7
Step by Step Guide and Essential Practice with Answers
Pre-Algebra
Ratio, Percent Proportion
Geometry
Statistics
MathFlare Publishing

MathFlare
MATH WORKBOOK
7-8
Step by Step Guide and Essential Practice with Answers
Pre-Algebra
Ratio, Percent Proportion
Geometry and Cartesian Plane
Statistics
MathFlare Publishing

MathFlare
MATH WORKBOOK
8-9
Step by Step Guide and Essential Practice with Answers
Pre-Algebra
Ratio, Proportion and Percentage
Linear Equations
Geometry and Cartesian Plane
MathFlare Publishing

MathFlare
MATH WORKBOOK
8
Step by Step Guide and Essential Practice with Answers
Pre-Algebra
Percentage
Linear Equations
Geometry
MathFlare Publishing

Place Value and Expanded Notations

Place value tells us the value of a digit in a number based on where it's placed.

Imagine we have the number 53. It has two digits: 5, and 3.

Now, each digit holds a special place:

The digit 5 is in the tens place. It means it's representing five groups of 10.

The digit 3 is in the ones place. It means it's representing three single units.

So, when we want to know the total value of the number 53, we add up the values of each digit based on its place value:

The digit 5 in the tens place is worth 50.

The digit 3 in the ones place is worth 3.

When we add these values together, we find the value of the entire number:

50 + 3 = 53

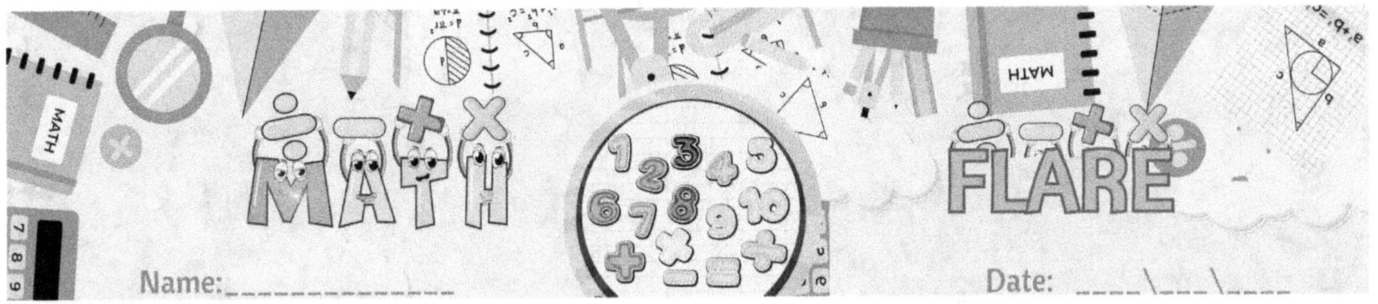

Place Value

Determine the place value of the underlined digit.

1. 237 = ___________________

2. 606 = ___________________

3. 224 = ___________________

4. 11 = ___________________

5. 221 = ___________________

6. 846 = ___________________

7. 597 = ___________________

8. 651 = ___________________

9. 482 = ___________________

10. 720 = ___________________

11. 687 = ___________________

12. 686 = ___________________

13. 899 = ___________________

14. 331 = ___________________

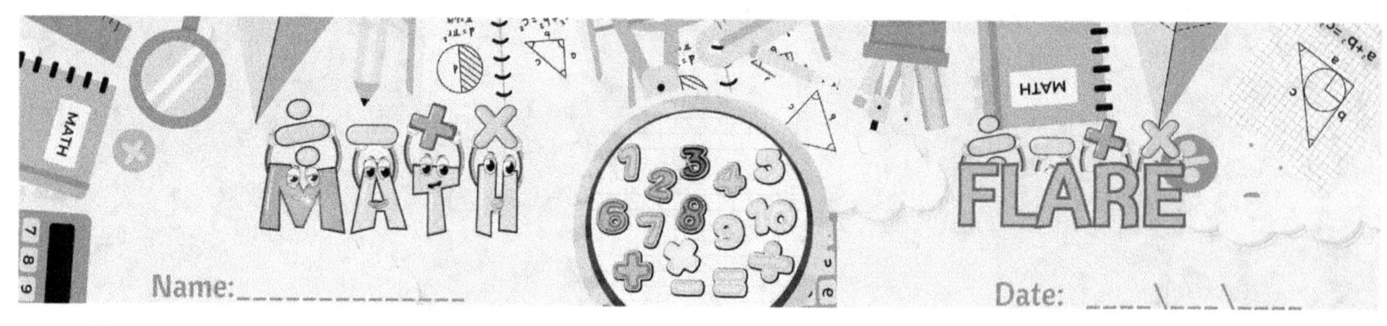

15. 5<u>5</u>9 = _________________________

16. 73<u>7</u> = _________________________

17. 58<u>3</u> = _________________________

18. <u>9</u>90 = _________________________

19. <u>5</u>1 = _________________________

20. 8<u>4</u>0 = _________________________

21. <u>2</u>01 = _________________________

22. 92<u>6</u> = _________________________

23. 14<u>4</u> = _________________________

24. <u>8</u>52 = _________________________

25. 73<u>8</u> = _________________________

26. 7<u>2</u>7 = _________________________

27. <u>7</u>16 = _________________________

28. <u>3</u>57 = _________________________

29. 41<u>9</u> = _________________________

30. 5<u>9</u>0 = _________________________

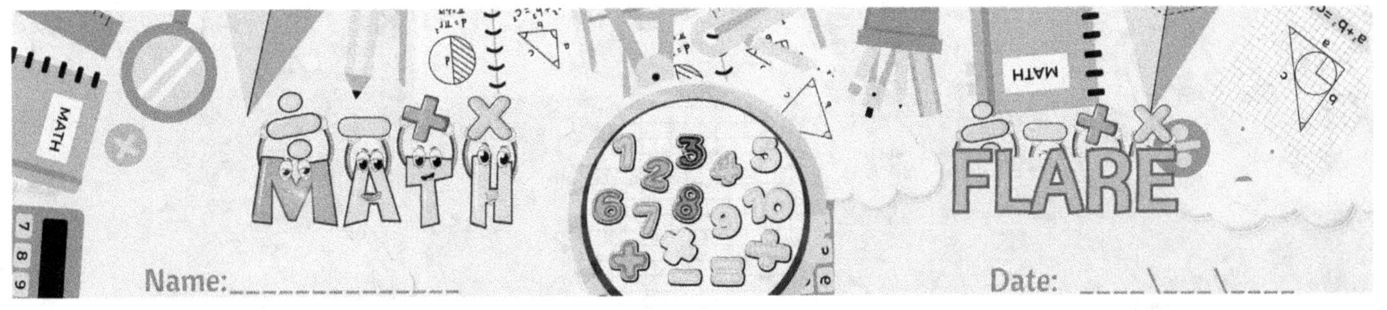

31. 3<u>2</u> = _______________________

32. 6<u>7</u>4 = _______________________

33. <u>4</u>05 = _______________________

34. 8<u>2</u>2 = _______________________

35. <u>6</u>33 = _______________________

36. 53<u>1</u> = _______________________

37. 82<u>8</u> = _______________________

38. 36<u>9</u> = _______________________

39. 27<u>3</u> = _______________________

40. <u>1</u>70 = _______________________

41. <u>9</u>72 = _______________________

42. 3<u>8</u>7 = _______________________

43. 29<u>1</u> = _______________________

44. <u>5</u>88 = _______________________

45. 7<u>97</u> = _______________________

46. 14<u>8</u> = _______________________

47. 5 6 3 = ___________________

48. 7 2 5 = ___________________

49. 7 7 8 = ___________________

50. 5 0 1 = ___________________

51. 2 7 7 = ___________________

52. 4 7 6 = ___________________

53. 9 8 1 = ___________________

54. 3 7 = ___________________

55. 6 7 9 = ___________________

56. 8 2 = ___________________

57. 1 5 8 = ___________________

58. 1 2 0 = ___________________

59. 8 8 0 = ___________________

60. 8 6 7 = ___________________

61. 2 3 3 = ___________________

62. 8 9 2 = ___________________

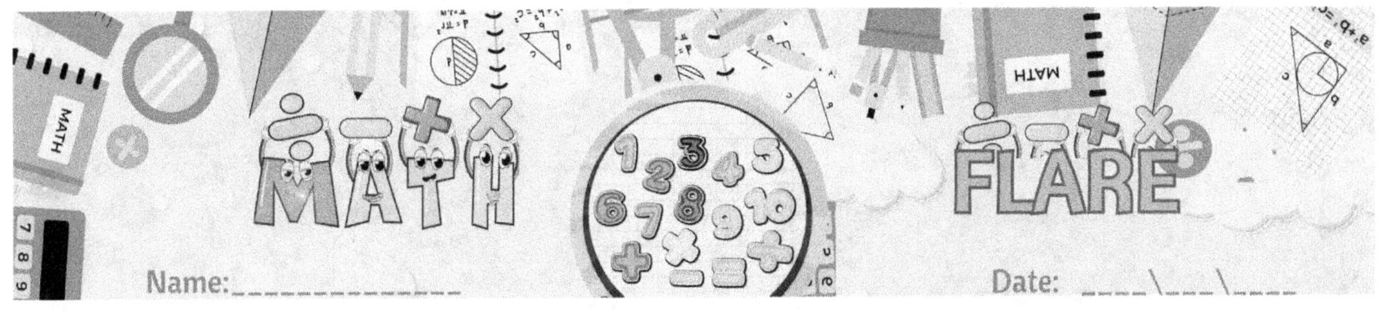

63. 6̲89 = __________________

64. 1̲4 = __________________

65. 2̲8̲2 = __________________

66. 7̲8̲ = __________________

67. 69̲7̲ = __________________

68. 2̲9̲ = __________________

69. 90̲7̲ = __________________

70. 2̲15 = __________________

71. 7̲18 = __________________

72. 81̲3̲ = __________________

73. 6̲3̲6 = __________________

74. 55̲5̲ = __________________

75. 5̲6 = __________________

76. 5̲9̲1 = __________________

77. 16̲5̲ = __________________

78. 9̲9̲1 = __________________

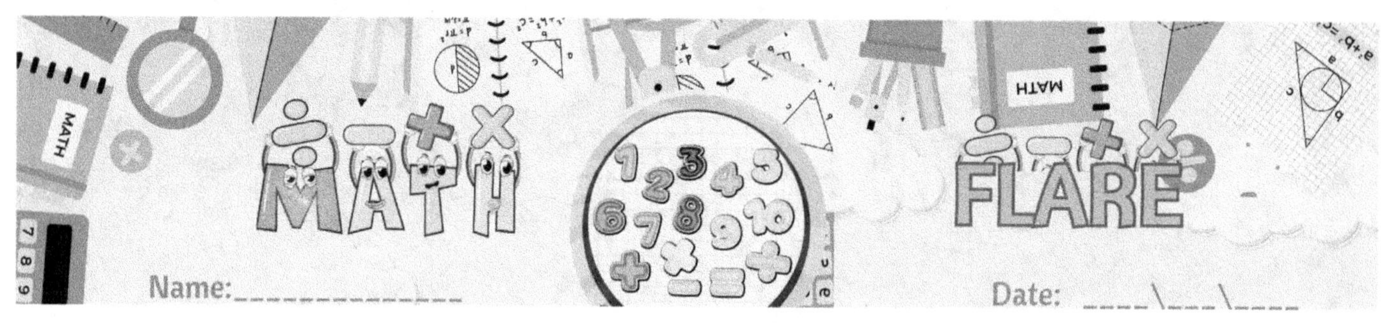

79. 578 = _______________________

80. 916 = _______________________

81. 314 = _______________________

82. 306 = _______________________

83. 423 = _______________________

84. 786 = _______________________

85. 953 = _______________________

86. 451 = _______________________

87. 671 = _______________________

88. 886 = _______________________

89. 154 = _______________________

90. 289 = _______________________

91. 106 = _______________________

92. 155 = _______________________

93. 398 = _______________________

94. 898 = _______________________

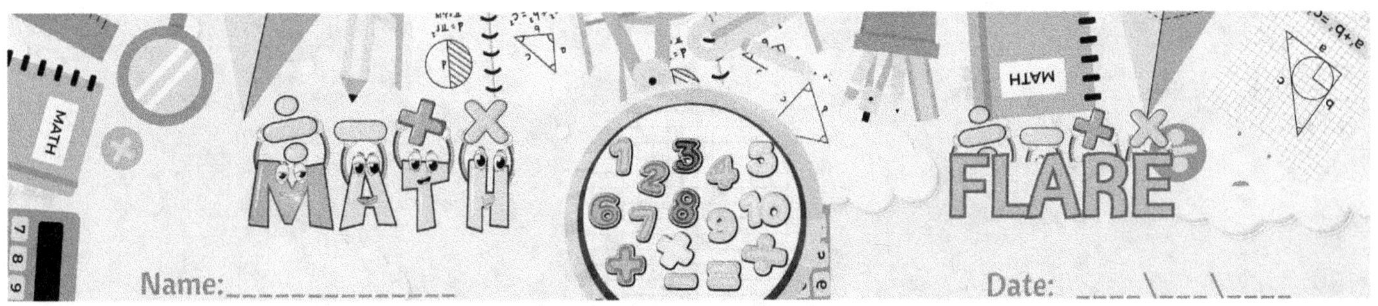

Place Value: Expanded Notation

Provide the expanded notation for each value.

95. __________ 6 tens + 5 ones

96. __________ 8 hundreds + 8 tens + 9 ones

97. __________ 9 hundreds + 2 ones

98. __________ 6 hundreds + 7 ones

99. __________ 2 hundreds + 7 ones

100. __________ 6 hundreds + 2 tens + 4 ones

101. __________ 4 hundreds + 4 tens + 3 ones

102. __________ 1 hundred + 7 tens + 1 one

103. __________ 9 hundreds + 9 ones

104. __________ 4 hundreds + 1 one

105. __________ 6 hundreds + 6 tens + 2 ones

106. __________ 1 ten + 6 ones

107. __________ 4 hundreds + 8 tens + 1 one

108. __________ 3 hundreds + 4 tens + 6 ones

109. __________ 2 hundreds + 7 tens + 8 ones

110. __________ 1 ten + 5 ones

111. __________ 2 hundreds + 4 tens + 7 ones

112. __________ 4 ones

113. __________ 7 hundreds + 5 tens + 5 ones

114. __________ 5 hundreds + 9 tens + 7 ones

115. __________ 2 hundreds + 4 tens + 1 one

116. __________ 5 hundreds + 1 ten + 8 ones

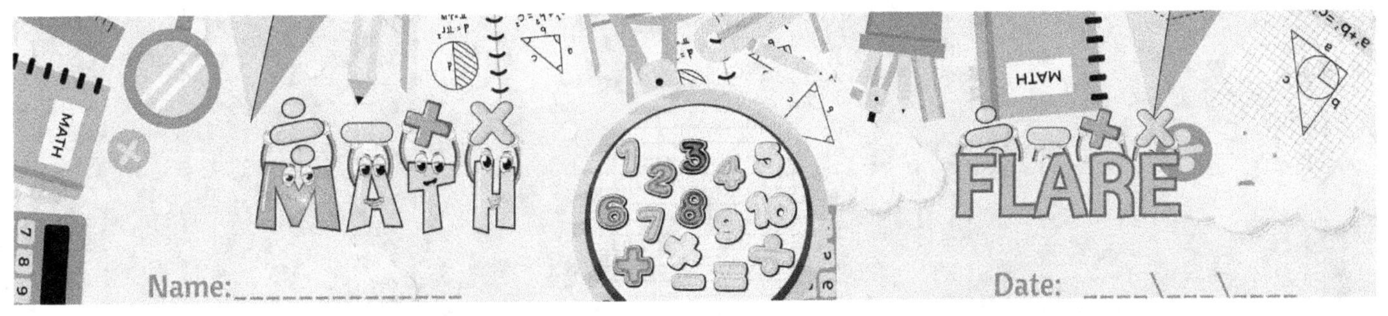

117. __________ 2 hundreds + 1 ten + 5 ones

118. __________ 8 hundreds + 4 ones

119. __________ 8 hundreds + 7 tens + 4 ones

120. __________ 5 tens + 2 ones

121. __________ 8 hundreds + 6 tens + 2 ones

122. __________ 4 hundreds + 2 tens + 8 ones

123. __________ 5 hundreds + 4 tens + 9 ones

124. __________ 2 hundreds + 7 tens + 3 ones

125. __________ 2 hundreds + 8 ones

126. __________ 5 tens + 8 ones

127. __________ 7 hundreds + 8 ones

128. __________ 7 hundreds + 5 ones

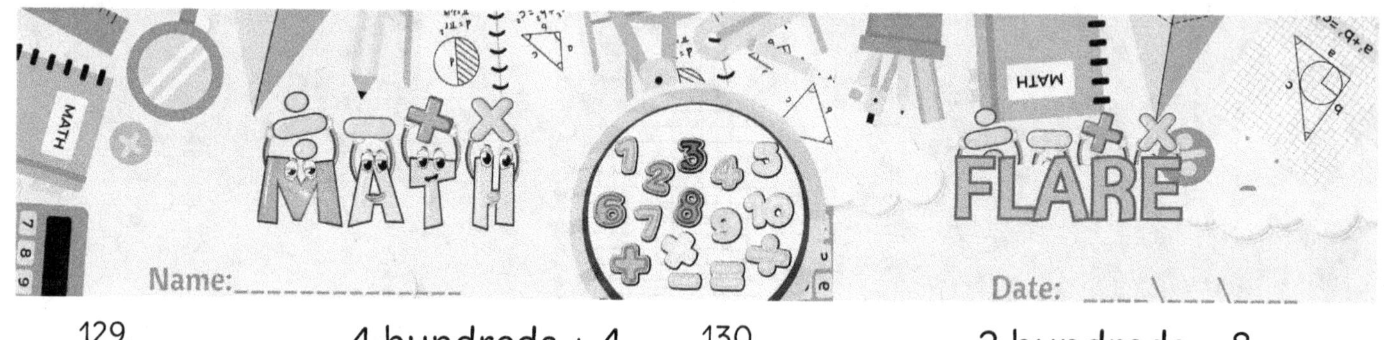

129. _________ 4 hundreds + 4 tens + 8 ones

130. _________ 2 hundreds + 8 tens

131. _________ 8 hundreds + 5 tens + 4 ones

132. _________ 9 hundreds + 1 ten + 3 ones

133. _________ 3 hundreds + 8 tens + 1 one

134. _________ 7 hundreds + 7 tens + 9 ones

135. _________ 8 hundreds + 4 tens + 1 one

136. _________ 1 hundred + 4 tens

137. _________ 7 hundreds + 5 tens + 7 ones

138. _________ 5 hundreds + 7 ones

139. _________ 8 hundreds + 1 ten + 5 ones

140. _________ 2 hundreds + 5 ones

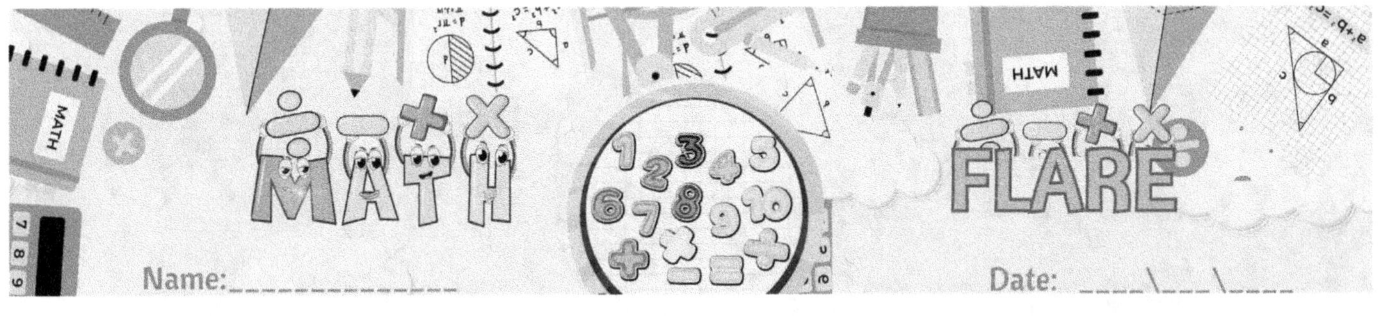

141. _____________ 4 hundreds + 2 tens

142. _____________ 8 hundreds + 2 tens + 7 ones

143. _____________ 6 hundreds + 1 one

144. _____________ 6 hundreds + 5 tens + 8 ones

145. _____________ 7 tens + 7 ones

146. _____________ 8 hundreds + 9 tens + 3 ones

147. _____________ 4 hundreds + 2 tens + 6 ones

148. _____________ 5 hundreds + 7 tens + 2 ones

149. _____________ 8 hundreds + 2 tens + 3 ones

150. _____________ 3 hundreds + 7 tens + 3 ones

151. _____________ 6 hundreds + 8 tens + 8 ones

152. _____________ 8 hundreds + 3 ones

153. __________ 3 hundreds + 3 tens + 1 one

154. __________ 5 hundreds + 7 tens + 3 ones

155. __________ 5 hundreds + 8 tens + 1 one

156. __________ 7 hundreds + 4 tens + 3 ones

157. __________ 3 hundreds + 6 tens + 1 one

158. __________ 1 hundred + 2 tens + 8 ones

159. __________ 4 hundreds + 5 tens + 5 ones

160. __________ 9 hundreds + 5 tens + 7 ones

161. __________ 7 hundreds + 7 tens + 2 ones

162. __________ 6 hundreds + 4 tens

163. __________ 8 hundreds + 2 tens + 9 ones

164. __________ 7 hundreds + 3 tens + 5 ones

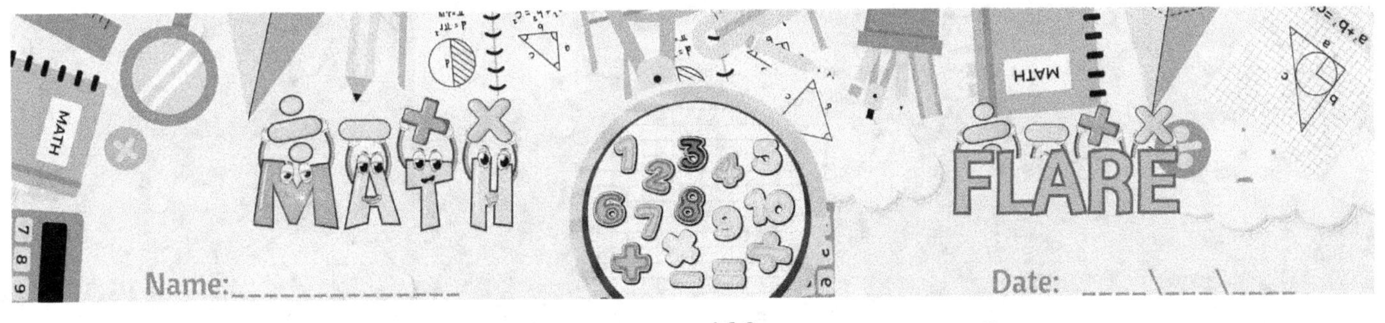

165. __________ 3 hundreds + 9 tens + 3 ones

166. __________ 9 tens

167. __________ 3 hundreds + 7 tens + 5 ones

168. __________ 9 hundreds + 7 tens + 4 ones

169. __________ 1 hundred + 2 ones

170. __________ 7 hundreds + 6 tens

171. __________ 7 hundreds + 7 ones

172. __________ 9 hundreds + 8 tens + 7 ones

173. __________ 6 hundreds + 7 tens

174. __________ 6 hundreds + 3 tens + 1 one

175. __________ 3 tens + 5 ones

176. __________ 8 hundreds + 2 tens + 6 ones

177. _________ 1 hundred + 9 tens + 7 ones

178. _________ 3 hundreds + 1 ten + 4 ones

179. _________ 1 hundred + 3 tens + 7 ones

180. _________ 8 hundreds + 8 tens + 1 one

181. _________ 7 tens + 6 ones

182. _________ 5 hundreds + 9 tens + 1 one

183. _________ 5 hundreds + 8 tens + 3 ones

184. _________ 8 hundreds + 7 ones

185. _________ 2 hundreds

186. _________ 9 tens + 9 ones

187. _________ 7 hundreds + 7 tens + 8 ones

188. _________ 6 hundreds + 3 tens

Place Value: Expanded Notation

Provide the expanded notation for each value.

189. 141 _______________________

190. 402 _______________________

191. 490 _______________________

192. 8 _______________________

193. 403 _______________________

194. 185 _______________________

195. 830 _______________________

196. 680 _______________________

197. 319 _______________________

198. 217 _______________________

199. 190 _______________

200. 527 _______________

201. 636 _______________

202. 749 _______________

203. 929 _______________

204. 698 _______________

205. 504 _______________

206. 623 _______________

207. 706 _______________

208. 445 _______________

209. 118 _______________

210. 208 _______________

211. 15 _______________________
____

212. 920 _______________________
____

213. 854 _______________________
____

214. 799 _______________________
____

215. 62 _______________________
____

216. 822 _______________________
____

217. 765 _______________________
____

218. 654 _______________________
____

219. 684 _______________________
____

220. 756 _______________________
____

221. 390 _______________________

222. 250 _______________________

223. 428 _______________________
____

224. 930 _______________________
____

225. 924 _______________________
____

226. 499 _______________________
____

227. 898 _______________________
____

228. 624 _______________________
____

229. 344 _______________________
____

230. 721 _______________________
____

231. 911 _______________________
____

232. 628 _______________________
____

233. 958 _______________________
____

234. 574 _______________________
____

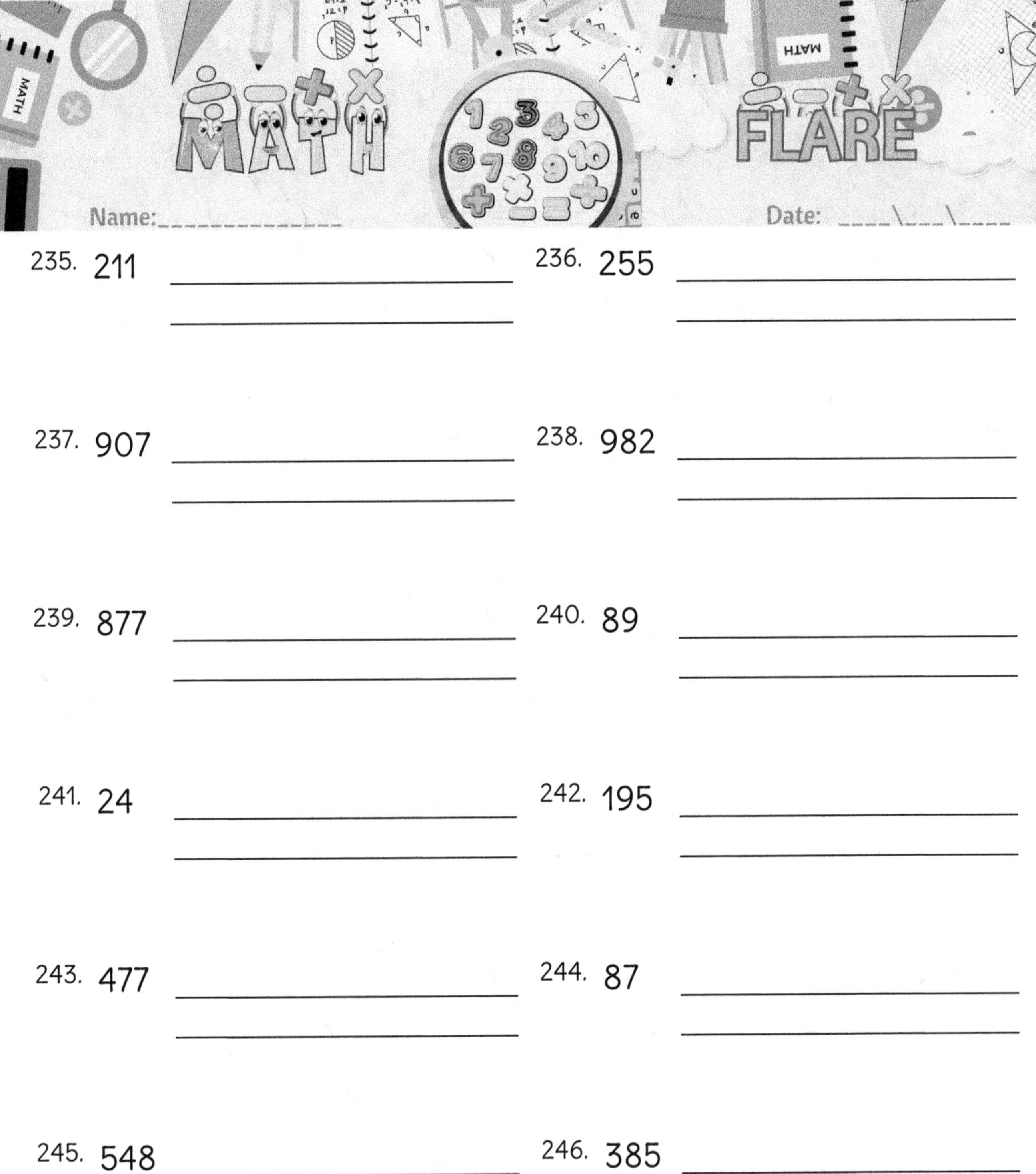

235. 211 ___________________
____

236. 255 ___________________
____

237. 907 ___________________
____

238. 982 ___________________
____

239. 877 ___________________
____

240. 89 ___________________
____

241. 24 ___________________
____

242. 195 ___________________
____

243. 477 ___________________
____

244. 87 ___________________
____

245. 548 ___________________
____

246. 385 ___________________
____

247. 946 ____________________

248. 1 ____________________

249. 857 ____________________

250. 553 ____________________

251. 563 ____________________

252. 505 ____________________

253. 769 ____________________

254. 247 ____________________

255. 500 ____________________

256. 502 ____________________

257. 767 ____________________

258. 580 ____________________

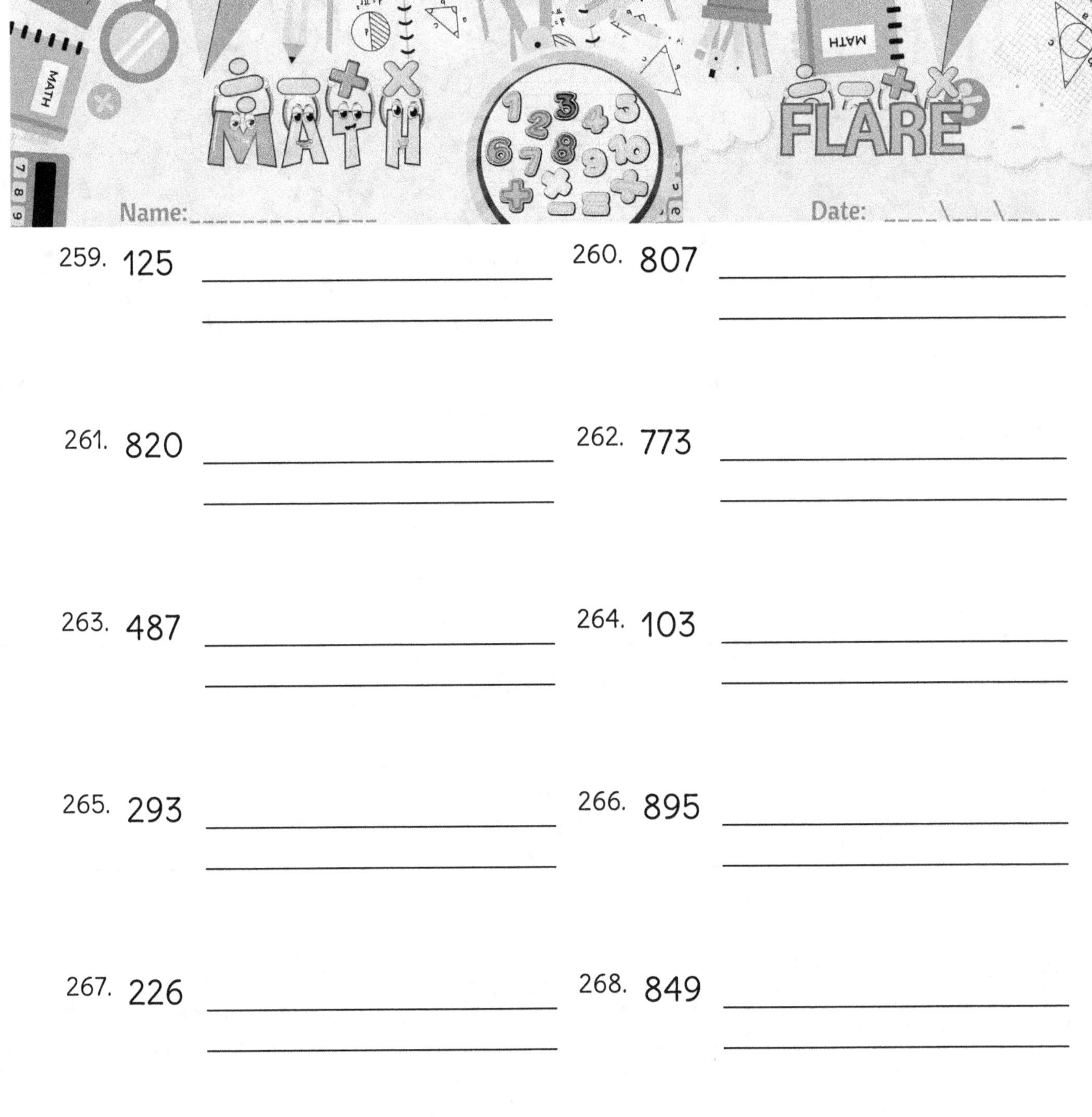

259. 125 ____________________
____

260. 807 ____________________
____

261. 820 ____________________
____

262. 773 ____________________
____

263. 487 ____________________
____

264. 103 ____________________
____

265. 293 ____________________
____

266. 895 ____________________
____

267. 226 ____________________
____

268. 849 ____________________
____

269. 576 ____________________
____

270. 58 ____________________
____

271. 856 ________________________

272. 670 ________________________

273. 806 ________________________

274. 668 ________________________

275. 367 ________________________

276. 56 ________________________

277. 950 ________________________

278. 844 ________________________

279. 377 ________________________

280. 116 ________________________

281. 951 ________________________

282. 486 ________________________

Place Value: Expanded Notation

Provide the expanded notation for each value.

283. _________ 800 + 8

284. _________ 400 + 50 + 6

285. _________ 800 + 50 + 8

286. _________ 800 + 9

287. _________ 100 + 60 + 4

288. _________ 400 + 30 + 6

289. _________ 800 + 20 + 3

290. _________ 900 + 30 + 2

291. _________ 100 + 60 + 7

292. _________ 30 + 4

293. _________ 600 + 10 + 5

294. _________ 300 + 30 + 5

295. _________ 800 + 80 + 4

296. _________ 700 + 10 + 6

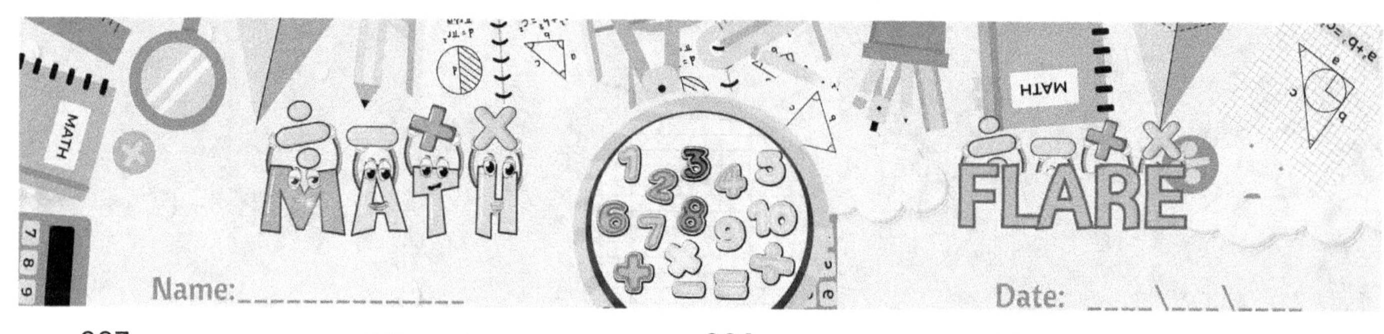

297. __________ 40 + 4

298. __________ 700 + 70 + 6

299. __________ 500 + 80 + 6

300. __________ 700 + 80 + 8

301. __________ 10 + 4

302. __________ 800 + 10 + 9

303. __________ 200 + 40 + 6

304. __________ 400 + 70 + 4

305. __________ 900 + 50 + 9

306. __________ 400 + 4

307. __________ 700 + 80 + 6

308. __________ 600 + 90 + 6

309. __________ 900 + 90 + 2

310. __________ 200 + 20 + 1

311. __________ 20 + 4

312. __________ 100 + 20 + 1

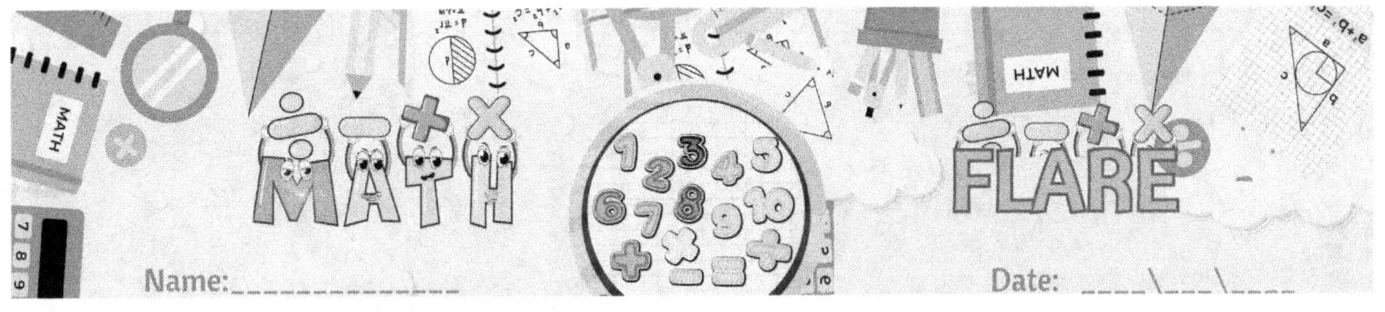

313. _________ 400 + 8

314. _________ 100 + 50

315. _________ 600 + 60 + 4

316. _________ 300 + 20 + 4

317. _________ 500 + 60 + 6

318. _________ 300 + 70 + 1

319. _________ 100 + 80

320. _________ 800 + 10 + 4

321. _________ 600 + 80 + 5

322. _________ 90 + 4

323. _________ 600 + 70 + 7

324. _________ 200 + 10 + 3

325. _________ 700 + 70 + 4

326. _________ 200 + 50 + 2

327. _________ 900 + 50 + 5

328. _________ 800 + 70 + 4

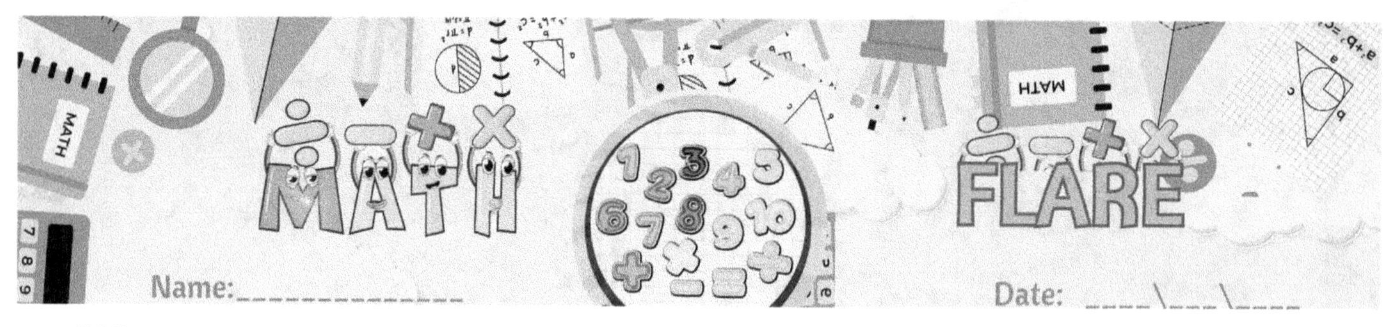

329. _________ 20 + 7

330. _________ 700 + 30 + 1

331. _________ 200 + 70 + 3

332. _________ 4

333. _________ 700 + 90 + 6

334. _________ 300 + 70 + 7

335. _________ 40 + 1

336. _________ 300 + 40 + 5

337. _________ 600 + 40 + 5

338. _________ 400 + 90 + 6

339. _________ 400 + 50 + 5

340. _________ 400 + 60 + 7

341. _________ 400 + 40 + 3

342. _________ 600 + 3

343. _________ 900 + 10

344. _________ 40 + 7

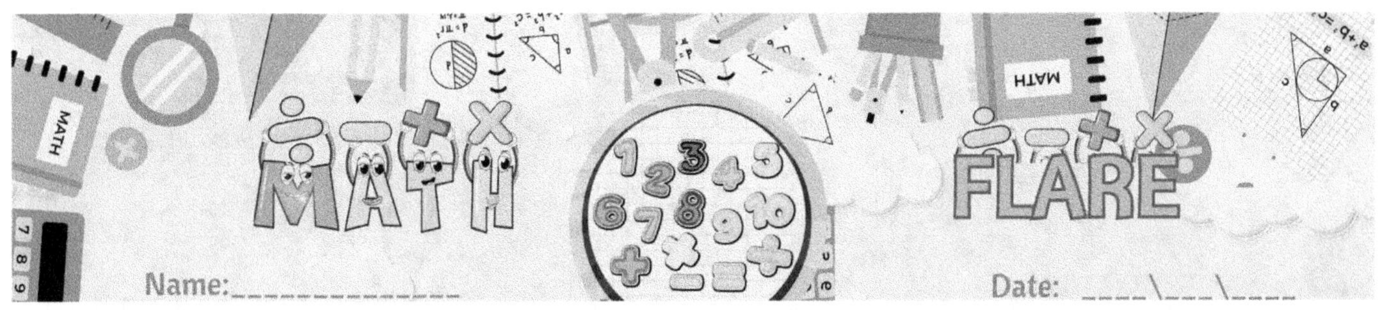

345. __________ 600 + 20 + 5

346. __________ 400 + 60 + 6

347. __________ 600 + 70

348. __________ 500 + 60 + 1

349. __________ 100 + 50 + 1

350. __________ 600 + 70 + 2

351. __________ 500 + 90 + 7

352. __________ 700 + 70 + 1

353. __________ 100 + 4

354. __________ 900 + 10 + 9

355. __________ 100 + 40 + 3

356. __________ 700

357. __________ 700 + 8

358. __________ 400 + 40 + 8

359. __________ 900 + 10 + 1

360. __________ 600 + 70 + 1

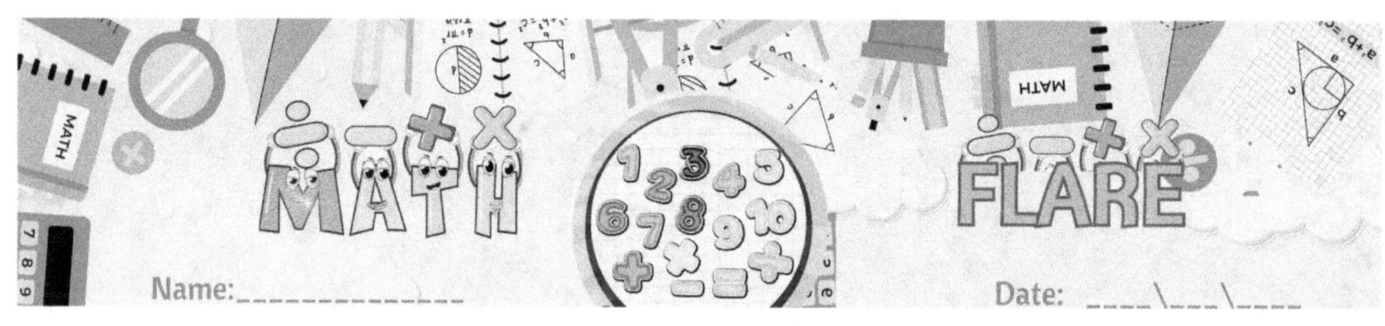

361. __________ 200 + 60 + 1

362. __________ 900 + 40 + 7

363. __________ 20

364. __________ 300 + 20 + 3

365. __________ 30 + 2

366. __________ 100 + 10

367. __________ 300 + 20

368. __________ 600 + 70 + 8

369. __________ 200 + 30 + 3

370. __________ 700 + 20 + 4

371. __________ 700 + 90 + 1

372. __________ 200 + 20

373. __________ 600 + 50

374. __________ 70 + 5

375. __________ 300 + 2

376. __________ 700 + 20 + 7

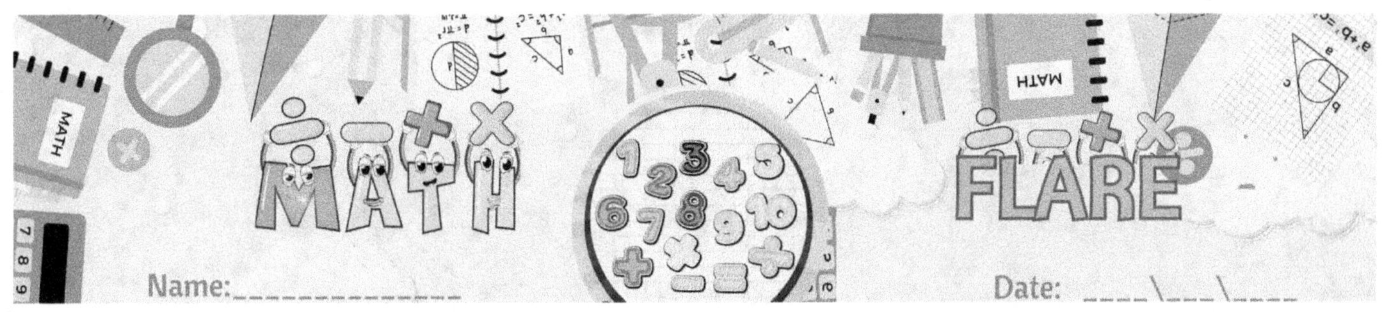

377. __________ 600 + 20 + 6

378. __________ 400 + 90

379. __________ 200 + 5

380. __________ 400 + 60 + 5

381. __________ 500 + 80 + 1

382. __________ 600

383. __________ 400 + 6

384. __________ 20 + 6

385. __________ 200 + 70 + 4

386. __________ 100 + 20 + 2

387. __________ 200 + 4

388. __________ 600 + 10 + 3

389. __________ 600 + 30 + 4

390. __________ 700 + 80 + 7

391. __________ 8

392. __________ 100 + 10 + 2

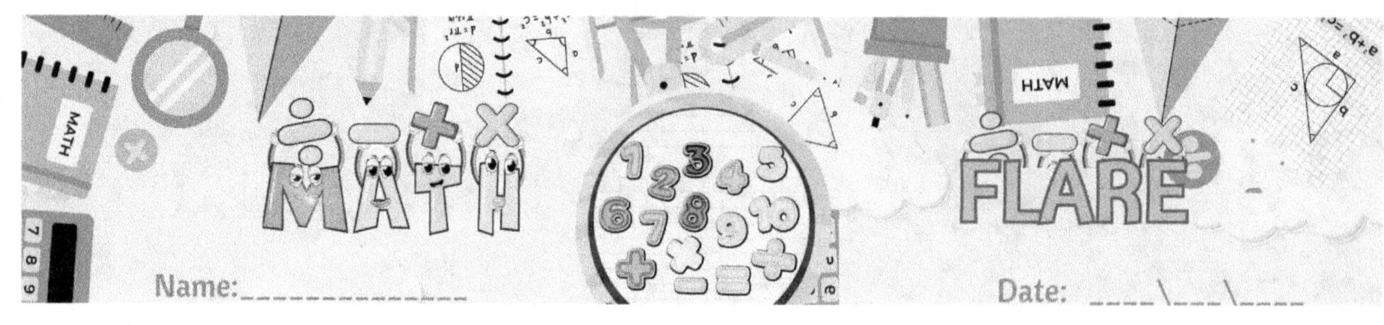

393. __________ 700 + 90 + 5

394. __________ 100 + 80 + 3

395. __________ 600 + 50 + 5

396. __________ 800 + 90

397. __________ 700 + 20 + 3

398. __________ 500 + 90 + 4

399. __________ 300 + 50 + 7

400. __________ 300 + 50 + 1

401. __________ 800 + 80 + 2

402. __________ 900 + 10 + 8

403. __________ 700 + 90 + 7

404. __________ 800 + 70 + 3

405. __________ 900 + 70 + 9

406. __________ 800 + 80 + 3

407. __________ 200 + 70

408. __________ 60 + 8

Place Value: Expanded Notation

Provide the expanded notation for each value.

409. 730 __________________

410. 971 __________________

411. 83 __________________

412. 956 __________________

413. 707 __________________

414. 207 __________________

415. 679 __________________

416. 348 __________________

417. 614 __________________

418. 298 __________________

419. 756 __________________

420. 987 __________________

421. 117 __________________

422. 66 __________________

423. 597 _______________________

424. 87 _______________________

425. 716 _______________________

426. 680 _______________________

427. 424 _______________________

428. 468 _______________________

429. 419 _______________________

430. 411 _______________________

431. 6 _______________________

432. 32 _______________________

433. 134 _______________________

434. 853 _______________________

435. 582 _______________________

436. 662 _______________________

437. 802 _______________________

438. 532 _______________________

439. 46 _______________

440. 390 _______________

441. 851 _______________

442. 136 _______________

443. 882 _______________

444. 705 _______________

445. 51 _______________

446. 403 _______________

447. 589 _______________

448. 502 _______________

449. 308 _______________

450. 278 _______________

451. 426 _______________

452. 837 _______________

453. 369 _______________

454. 235 _______________

MathFlare -Place Value and Expanded Notations 1st Grade

455. 817 ___________________

456. 321 ___________________

457. 711 ___________________

458. 158 ___________________

459. 301 ___________________

460. 460 ___________________

461. 801 ___________________

462. 648 ___________________

463. 320 ___________________

464. 967 ___________________

465. 52 ___________________

466. 823 ___________________

467. 624 ___________________

468. 18 ___________________

469. 545 ___________________

470. 82 ___________________

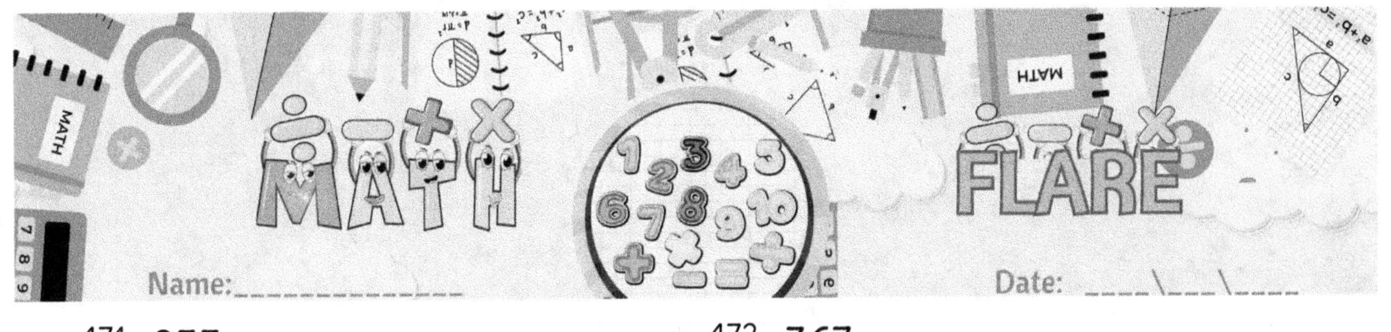

471. 253 _______________________

472. 367 _______________________

473. 137 _______________________

474. 980 _______________________

475. 183 _______________________

476. 935 _______________________

477. 381 _______________________

478. 666 _______________________

479. 833 _______________________

480. 965 _______________________

481. 112 _______________________

482. 579 _______________________

483. 194 _______________________

484. 764 _______________________

485. 620 _______________________

486. 342 _______________________

487. 92 ________________________

488. 375 ________________________

489. 744 ________________________

490. 929 ________________________

491. 488 ________________________

492. 563 ________________________

493. 694 ________________________

494. 654 ________________________

495. 227 ________________________

496. 549 ________________________

497. 485 ________________________

498. 763 ________________________

499. 196 ________________________

500. 174 ________________________

501. 471 ________________________

502. 233 ________________________

503. 254 _______________________

504. 634 _______________________

505. 385 _______________________

506. 330 _______________________

507. 491 _______________________

508. 24 _______________________

509. 626 _______________________

510. 835 _______________________

511. 537 _______________________

512. 187 _______________________

513. 389 _______________________

514. 857 _______________________

515. 60 _______________________

516. 859 _______________________

517. 675 _______________________

518. 453 _______________________

519. 706 _______________ 520. 508 _______________

521. 437 _______________ 522. 493 _______________

523. 242 _______________ 524. 727 _______________

525. 440 _______________ 526. 728 _______________

527. 868 _______________ 528. 480 _______________

529. 349 _______________ 530. 937 _______________

531. 406 _______________ 532. 722 _______________

533. 131 _______________ 534. 761 _______________

535. 884 _________________________

536. 304 _________________________

537. 216 _________________________

538. 950 _________________________

539. 377 _________________________

540. 306 _________________________

541. 796 _________________________

542. 167 _________________________

543. 316 _________________________

544. 107 _________________________

545. 810 _________________________

546. 310 _________________________

547. 489 _________________________

548. 665 _________________________

549. 35 _________________________

550. 147 _________________________

Place Value: Expanded Notation

Provide the expanded notation for each value.

551. __________ seven hundred fifty-nine

552. __________ sixteen

553. __________ one hundred forty-four

554. __________ six hundred three

555. __________ fifty-one

556. __________ two hundred ninety-five

557. __________ seven hundred fifty-eight

558. __________ three hundred fifty-five

559. __________ one hundred eighty-nine

560. __________ two hundred forty-eight

Name:__________________

Date: ____________

561. __________ nine hundred eighty-two

562. __________ one hundred thirty-six

563. __________ five hundred twenty-eight

564. __________ eight hundred sixty-seven

565. __________ seven hundred twenty-nine

566. __________ seven hundred eighteen

567. __________ six hundred ninety-two

568. __________ eight hundred twenty-one

569. __________ seven hundred eighty-five

570. __________ one hundred thirty-four

571. __________ eight hundred seventy

572. __________ five hundred forty-two

573. __________ two hundred forty-three

574. __________ nine hundred thirty-five

575. __________ nine hundred thirty

576. __________ two hundred seventy-four

577. __________ four hundred thirteen

578. __________ seven hundred sixty-two

579. __________ six hundred seventy

580. __________ forty

581. __________ four hundred forty-nine

582. __________ seven hundred thirty-nine

583. __________ six hundred eighty-eight

584. __________ three hundred eighty-five

585. __________ six hundred seven

586. __________ one hundred sixteen

587. __________ eight hundred thirteen

588. __________ one hundred fifty -nine

589. __________ eight hundred thirty-three

590. __________ four hundred twenty-seven

591. __________ five hundred forty-five

592. __________ eight hundred fifty-nine

593. __________ one hundred thirty

594. __________ three hundred twenty-two

595. __________ six hundred sixty -one

596. __________ six hundred thirty-nine

597. __________ four hundred forty-eight

598. __________ three hundred seventy-seven

599. __________ ninety-three

600. __________ six hundred seventeen

601. __________ six hundred sixty -seven

602. __________ eight hundred seventy-nine

603. __________ nine hundred one

604. __________ two hundred seventy-six

605. __________ two hundred eighteen

606. __________ seven hundred seventy-two

607. __________ two hundred nine

608. __________ six hundred seventy-two

609. _________ seven hundred seventy-seven

610. _________ eight hundred eighty-one

611. _________ nine hundred ninety-five

612. _________ six hundred eighty-five

613. _________ one hundred fifty

614. _________ seven hundred ninety-nine

615. _________ two hundred forty-four

616. _________ four hundred forty-seven

617. _________ one hundred forty-three

618. _________ two hundred sixty-one

619. _________ six hundred fourteen

620. _________ nine hundred four

621. __________ five hundred thirty-four

622. __________ nine hundred eighty-seven

623. __________ three hundred fifty-nine

624. __________ five hundred eighty-seven

625. __________ twelve

626. __________ seven hundred seventy-nine

627. __________ one hundred fifteen

628. __________ two hundred sixty-nine

629. __________ six hundred thirty-four

630. __________ nine hundred sixty-four

631. __________ three hundred eighty-six

632. __________ five hundred seventy-seven

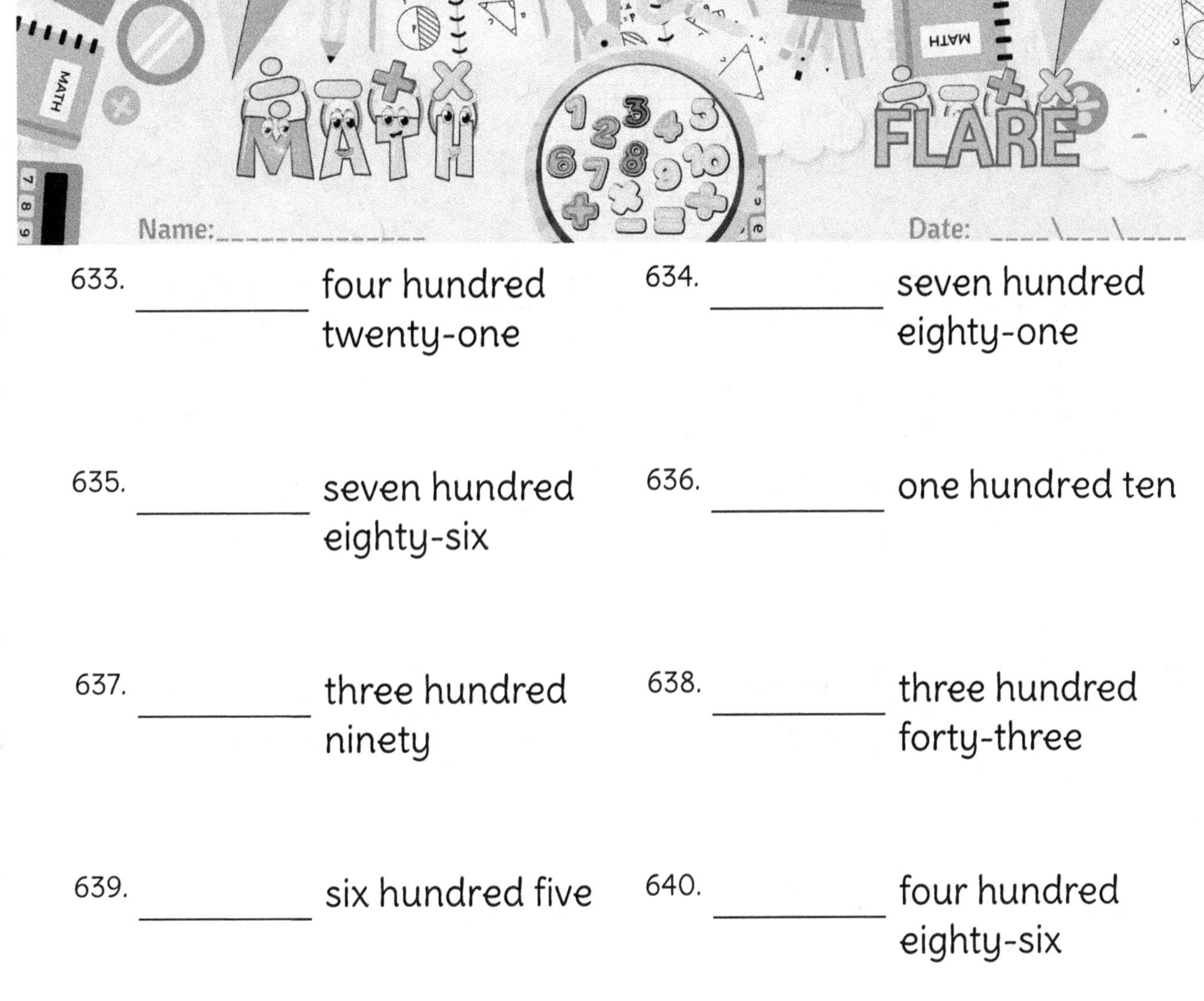

633. __________ four hundred twenty-one

634. __________ seven hundred eighty-one

635. __________ seven hundred eighty-six

636. __________ one hundred ten

637. __________ three hundred ninety

638. __________ three hundred forty-three

639. __________ six hundred five

640. __________ four hundred eighty-six

641. __________ fifty-eight

642. __________ five hundred forty-nine

643. __________ one hundred seventy-five

644. __________ six hundred thirteen

645. __________ three hundred thirty

646. __________ seventy-nine

647. __________ two hundred sixteen

648. __________ four hundred ninety-seven

649. __________ one hundred eighty-eight

650. __________ seven hundred sixty-one

651. __________ eighty-five

652. __________ six hundred seventy-nine

653. __________ five hundred twenty-two

654. __________ three hundred fourteen

655. __________ two hundred sixty-five

656. __________ four hundred thirty-eight

657. __________ six hundred fifty-eight

658. __________ five hundred ninety-four

659. __________ four hundred four

660. __________ nine hundred sixteen

661. __________ six hundred ten

662. __________ one hundred nine

663. __________ seven hundred twenty-eight

664. __________ eighteen

665. __________ six hundred fifty-nine

666. __________ thirty-four

667. __________ two hundred seventy-two

668. __________ three hundred

669. __________ forty-nine

670. __________ thirty-nine

671. __________ eight hundred thirty-six

672. __________ one hundred sixty-six

673. __________ seven hundred eighty-three

674. __________ five hundred thirty-five

675. __________ fifty-five

676. __________ one hundred thirty-eight

677. __________ six hundred twenty-four

678. __________ three hundred thirty-eight

679. __________ one hundred four

680. __________ four hundred seventy-three

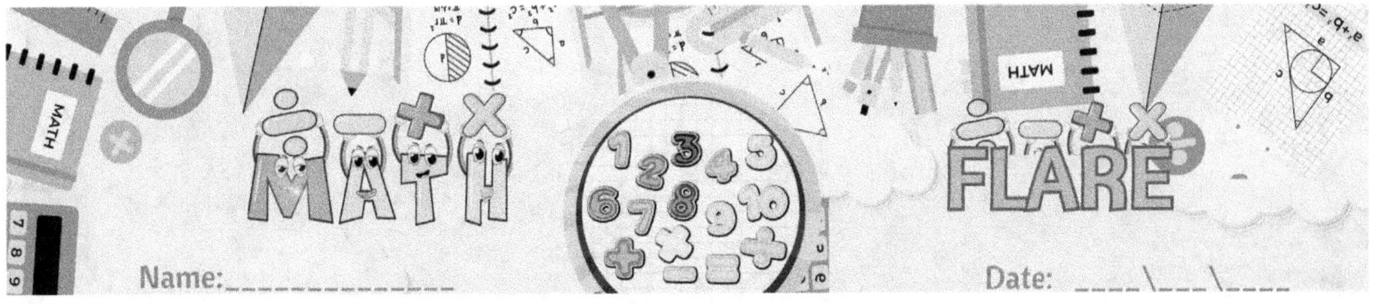

Place Value: Expanded Notation

Provide the expanded notation for each value.

681. 85 _______________________

682. 95 _______________________

683. 69 _______________________

684. 2 _______________________

685. 9 _______________________

686. 91 _______________________

687. 63 _______________________

688. 94 _______________________

689. 8 _______________________

690. 89 _______________________

691. 32 _______________________

692. 70 _______________________

693. 56 _______________________

694. 47 _______________________

695. 49 _______________

696. 5 _______________

697. 75 _______________

698. 71 _______________

699. 28 _______________

700. 43 _______________

701. 88 _______________

702. 7 _______________

703. 36 _______________

704. 15 _______________

705. 99 _______________

706. 72 _______________

707. 40 _______________

708. 92 _______________

709. 6 _______________

710. 19 _______________

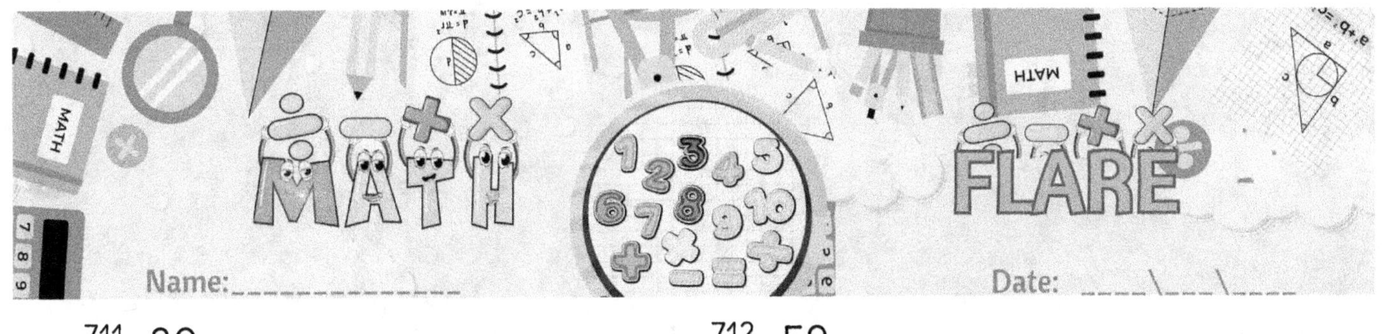

711. 20 ______________________   712. 59 ______________________

713. 30 ______________________   714. 97 ______________________

715. 3 ______________________   716. 11 ______________________

717. 77 ______________________   718. 29 ______________________

719. 48 ______________________   720. 84 ______________________

721. 50 ______________________   722. 68 ______________________

723. 14 ______________________   724. 51 ______________________

725. 31 ______________________   726. 21 ______________________

727. 42 _______________________

728. 81 _______________________

729. 74 _______________________

730. 65 _______________________

731. 37 _______________________

732. 90 _______________________

733. 60 _______________________

734. 73 _______________________

735. 53 _______________________

736. 18 _______________________

737. 66 _______________________

738. 41 _______________________

739. 22 _______________________

740. 34 _______________________

741. 10 _______________________

742. 78 _______________________

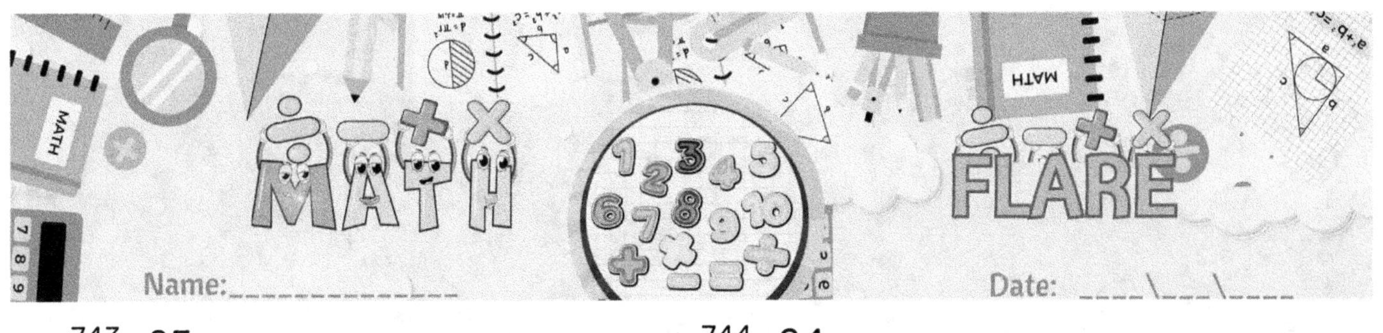

743. 25 _________________________

744. 24 _________________________

745. 12 _________________________

746. 79 _________________________

747. 76 _________________________

748. 58 _________________________

749. 39 _________________________

750. 16 _________________________

751. 13 _________________________

752. 27 _________________________

753. 62 _________________________

754. 83 _________________________

755. 4 _________________________

756. 93 _________________________

757. 86 _________________________

758. 38 _________________________

759. 54 ___________________

760. 96 ___________________

761. 64 ___________________

762. 1 ___________________

763. 17 ___________________

764. 82 ___________________

765. 67 ___________________

766. 98 ___________________

767. 52 ___________________

768. 46 ___________________

769. 57 ___________________

770. 35 ___________________

771. 61 ___________________

772. 44 ___________________

773. 55 ___________________

774. 100 ___________________

ANSWERS

Page 1: Place Value

1. 7 ones
2. 6 ones
3. 2 tens
4. 1 ten
5. 1 one
6. 4 tens
7. 5 hundreds
8. 1 one
9. 8 tens
10. 7 hundreds
11. 6 hundreds
12. 6 hundreds
13. 9 tens
14. 3 hundreds
15. 9 ones
16. 7 ones
17. 3 ones
18. 9 hundreds
19. 5 tens
20. 4 tens
21. 2 hundreds
22. 6 ones
23. 4 ones
24. 8 hundreds
25. 8 ones
26. 2 tens
27. 7 hundreds
28. 3 hundreds
29. 1 ten
30. 9 tens
31. 2 ones
32. 7 tens
33. 4 hundreds
34. 2 tens
35. 6 hundreds
36. 1 one
37. 8 ones
38. 9 ones
39. 3 ones
40. 1 hundred
41. 9 hundreds
42. 7 ones
43. 1 one
44. 5 hundreds
45. 9 tens
46. 8 ones
47. 3 ones
48. 2 tens
49. 8 ones
50. 5 hundreds
51. 7 tens
52. 6 ones
53. 1 one
54. 7 ones
55. 9 ones
56. 8 tens
57. 1 hundred
58. 1 hundred
59. 8 hundreds
60. 8 hundreds
61. 3 tens
62. 2 ones
63. 6 hundreds
64. 4 ones
65. 8 tens
66. 8 ones
67. 7 ones
68. 9 ones
69. 7 ones
70. 2 hundreds
71. 7 hundreds
72. 3 ones
73. 3 tens
74. 5 ones
75. 5 tens
76. 9 tens

77. 5 ones   78. 9 tens   79. 8 ones   80. 6 ones

81. 1 ten   82. 6 ones   83. 4 hundreds   84. 8 tens

85. 9 hundreds   86. 1 one   87. 1 one   88. 8 tens

89. 4 ones   90. 2 hundreds   91. 6 ones   92. 5 tens

93. 8 ones   94. 9 tens

Page 7: Place Value: Expanded Notation

95. 65	96. 889	97. 902	98. 607	99. 207	100. 624
101. 443	102. 171	103. 909	104. 401	105. 662	106. 16
107. 481	108. 346	109. 278	110. 15	111. 247	112. 4
113. 755	114. 597	115. 241	116. 518	117. 215	118. 804
119. 874	120. 52	121. 862	122. 428	123. 549	124. 273
125. 208	126. 58	127. 708	128. 705	129. 448	130. 280
131. 854	132. 913	133. 381	134. 779	135. 841	136. 140
137. 757	138. 507	139. 815	140. 205	141. 420	142. 827
143. 601	144. 658	145. 77	146. 893	147. 426	148. 572
149. 823	150. 373	151. 688	152. 803	153. 331	154. 573
155. 581	156. 743	157. 361	158. 128	159. 455	160. 957
161. 772	162. 640	163. 829	164. 735	165. 393	166. 90
167. 375	168. 974	169. 102	170. 760	171. 707	172. 987
173. 670	174. 631	175. 35	176. 826	177. 197	178. 314
179. 137	180. 881	181. 76	182. 591	183. 583	184. 807

185. 200   186. 99   187. 778   188. 630

Page 15: Place Value: Expanded Notation

189. 1 hundred + 4 tens + 1 one

190. 4 hundreds + 2 ones

191. 4 hundreds + 9 tens

192. 8 ones

193. 4 hundreds + 3 ones

194. 1 hundred + 8 tens + 5 ones

195. 8 hundreds + 3 tens

196. 6 hundreds + 8 tens

197. 3 hundreds + 1 ten + 9 ones

198. 2 hundreds + 1 ten + 7 ones

199. 1 hundred + 9 tens

200. 5 hundreds + 2 tens + 7 ones

201. 6 hundreds + 3 tens + 6 ones

202. 7 hundreds + 4 tens + 9 ones

203. 9 hundreds + 2 tens + 9 ones

204. 6 hundreds + 9 tens + 8 ones

205. 5 hundreds + 4 ones

206. 6 hundreds + 2 tens + 3 ones

207. 7 hundreds + 6 ones

208. 4 hundreds + 4 tens + 5 ones

209. 1 hundred + 1 ten + 8 ones

210. 2 hundreds + 8 ones

211. 1 ten + 5 ones

212. 9 hundreds + 2 tens

213. 8 hundreds + 5 tens + 4 ones

214. 7 hundreds + 9 tens + 9 ones

215. 6 tens + 2 ones

216. 8 hundreds + 2 tens + 2 ones

217. 7 hundreds + 6 tens + 5 ones

218. 6 hundreds + 5 tens + 4 ones

219. 6 hundreds + 8 tens + 4 ones

220. 7 hundreds + 5 tens + 6 ones

221. 3 hundreds + 9 tens

222. 2 hundreds + 5 tens

223. 4 hundreds + 2 tens + 8 ones

224. 9 hundreds + 3 tens

225. 9 hundreds + 2 tens + 4 ones

226. 4 hundreds + 9 tens + 9 ones

227. 8 hundreds + 9 tens + 8 ones

228. 6 hundreds + 2 tens + 4 ones

229. 3 hundreds + 4 tens + 4 ones

230. 7 hundreds + 2 tens + 1 one

231. 9 hundreds + 1 ten + 1 one

232. 6 hundreds + 2 tens + 8 ones

233. 9 hundreds + 5 tens + 8 ones

234. 5 hundreds + 7 tens + 4 ones

235. 2 hundreds + 1 ten + 1 one

236. 2 hundreds + 5 tens + 5 ones

237. 9 hundreds + 7 ones

238. 9 hundreds + 8 tens + 2 ones

239. 8 hundreds + 7 tens + 7 ones

240. 8 tens + 9 ones

241. 2 tens + 4 ones

242. 1 hundred + 9 tens + 5 ones

243. 4 hundreds + 7 tens + 7 ones

244. 8 tens + 7 ones

245. 5 hundreds + 4 tens + 8 ones

246. 3 hundreds + 8 tens + 5 ones

247. 9 hundreds + 4 tens + 6 ones

248. 1 one

249. 8 hundreds + 5 tens + 7 ones

250. 5 hundreds + 5 tens + 3 ones

251. 5 hundreds + 6 tens + 3 ones

252. 5 hundreds + 5 ones

253. 7 hundreds + 6 tens + 9 ones

254. 2 hundreds + 4 tens + 7 ones

255. 5 hundreds

256. 5 hundreds + 2 ones

257. 7 hundreds + 6 tens + 7 ones

258. 5 hundreds + 8 tens

259. 1 hundred + 2 tens + 5 ones

260. 8 hundreds + 7 ones

261. 8 hundreds + 2 tens

262. 7 hundreds + 7 tens + 3 ones

263. 4 hundreds + 8 tens + 7 ones

264. 1 hundred + 3 ones

265. 2 hundreds + 9 tens + 3 ones

266. 8 hundreds + 9 tens + 5 ones

267. 2 hundreds + 2 tens + 6 ones

268. 8 hundreds + 4 tens + 9 ones

269. 5 hundreds + 7 tens + 6 ones   270. 5 tens + 8 ones

271. 8 hundreds + 5 tens + 6 ones   272. 6 hundreds + 7 tens

273. 8 hundreds + 6 ones   274. 6 hundreds + 6 tens + 8 ones

275. 3 hundreds + 6 tens + 7 ones   276. 5 tens + 6 ones

277. 9 hundreds + 5 tens   278. 8 hundreds + 4 tens + 4 ones

279. 3 hundreds + 7 tens + 7 ones   280. 1 hundred + 1 ten + 6 ones

281. 9 hundreds + 5 tens + 1 one   282. 4 hundreds + 8 tens + 6 ones

Page 23: Place Value: Expanded Notation

283. 808	284. 456	285. 858	286. 809	287. 164	288. 436
289. 823	290. 932	291. 167	292. 34	293. 615	294. 335
295. 884	296. 716	297. 44	298. 776	299. 586	300. 788
301. 14	302. 819	303. 246	304. 474	305. 959	306. 404
307. 786	308. 696	309. 992	310. 221	311. 24	312. 121
313. 408	314. 150	315. 664	316. 324	317. 566	318. 371
319. 180	320. 814	321. 685	322. 94	323. 677	324. 213
325. 774	326. 252	327. 955	328. 874	329. 27	330. 731
331. 273	332. 4	333. 796	334. 377	335. 41	336. 345
337. 645	338. 496	339. 455	340. 467	341. 443	342. 603
343. 910	344. 47	345. 625	346. 466	347. 670	348. 561
349. 151	350. 672	351. 597	352. 771	353. 104	354. 919
355. 143	356. 700	357. 708	358. 448	359. 911	360. 671

361. 261	362. 947	363. 20	364. 323	365. 32	366. 110
367. 320	368. 678	369. 233	370. 724	371. 791	372. 220
373. 650	374. 75	375. 302	376. 727	377. 626	378. 490
379. 205	380. 465	381. 581	382. 600	383. 406	384. 26
385. 274	386. 122	387. 204	388. 613	389. 634	390. 787
391. 8	392. 112	393. 795	394. 183	395. 655	396. 890
397. 723	398. 594	399. 357	400. 351	401. 882	402. 918
403. 797	404. 873	405. 979	406. 883	407. 270	408. 68

Page 31:   Place Value: Expanded Notation

409. 700 + 30	410. 900 + 70 + 1	411. 80 + 3
412. 900 + 50 + 6	413. 700 + 7	414. 200 + 7
415. 600 + 70 + 9	416. 300 + 40 + 8	417. 600 + 10 + 4
418. 200 + 90 + 8	419. 700 + 50 + 6	420. 900 + 80 + 7
421. 100 + 10 + 7	422. 60 + 6	423. 500 + 90 + 7
424. 80 + 7	425. 700 + 10 + 6	426. 600 + 80
427. 400 + 20 + 4	428. 400 + 60 + 8	429. 400 + 10 + 9
430. 400 + 10 + 1	431. 6	432. 30 + 2
433. 100 + 30 + 4	434. 800 + 50 + 3	435. 500 + 80 + 2
436. 600 + 60 + 2	437. 800 + 2	438. 500 + 30 + 2
439. 40 + 6	440. 300 + 90	441. 800 + 50 + 1
442. 100 + 30 + 6	443. 800 + 80 + 2	444. 700 + 5

445. 50 + 1

446. 400 + 3

447. 500 + 80 + 9

448. 500 + 2

449. 300 + 8

450. 200 + 70 + 8

451. 400 + 20 + 6

452. 800 + 30 + 7

453. 300 + 60 + 9

454. 200 + 30 + 5

455. 800 + 10 + 7

456. 300 + 20 + 1

457. 700 + 10 + 1

458. 100 + 50 + 8

459. 300 + 1

460. 400 + 60

461. 800 + 1

462. 600 + 40 + 8

463. 300 + 20

464. 900 + 60 + 7

465. 50 + 2

466. 800 + 20 + 3

467. 600 + 20 + 4

468. 10 + 8

469. 500 + 40 + 5

470. 80 + 2

471. 200 + 50 + 3

472. 300 + 60 + 7

473. 100 + 30 + 7

474. 900 + 80

475. 100 + 80 + 3

476. 900 + 30 + 5

477. 300 + 80 + 1

478. 600 + 60 + 6

479. 800 + 30 + 3

480. 900 + 60 + 5

481. 100 + 10 + 2

482. 500 + 70 + 9

483. 100 + 90 + 4

484. 700 + 60 + 4

485. 600 + 20

486. 300 + 40 + 2

487. 90 + 2

488. 300 + 70 + 5

489. 700 + 40 + 4

490. 900 + 20 + 9

491. 400 + 80 + 8

492. 500 + 60 + 3

493. 600 + 90 + 4

494. 600 + 50 + 4

495. 200 + 20 + 7

496. 500 + 40 + 9

497. 400 + 80 + 5

498. 700 + 60 + 3

499. 100 + 90 + 6

500. 100 + 70 + 4

501. 400 + 70 + 1

502. 200 + 30 + 3

503. 200 + 50 + 4

504. 600 + 30 + 4

505. 300 + 80 + 5

506. 300 + 30

507. 400 + 90 + 1

508. 20 + 4   509. 600 + 20 + 6   510. 800 + 30 + 5

511. 500 + 30 + 7   512. 100 + 80 + 7   513. 300 + 80 + 9

514. 800 + 50 + 7   515. 60   516. 800 + 50 + 9

517. 600 + 70 + 5   518. 400 + 50 + 3   519. 700 + 6

520. 500 + 8   521. 400 + 30 + 7   522. 400 + 90 + 3

523. 200 + 40 + 2   524. 700 + 20 + 7   525. 400 + 40

526. 700 + 20 + 8   527. 800 + 60 + 8   528. 400 + 80

529. 300 + 40 + 9   530. 900 + 30 + 7   531. 400 + 6

532. 700 + 20 + 2   533. 100 + 30 + 1   534. 700 + 60 + 1

535. 800 + 80 + 4   536. 300 + 4   537. 200 + 10 + 6

538. 900 + 50   539. 300 + 70 + 7   540. 300 + 6

541. 700 + 90 + 6   542. 100 + 60 + 7   543. 300 + 10 + 6

544. 100 + 7   545. 800 + 10   546. 300 + 10

547. 400 + 80 + 9   548. 600 + 60 + 5   549. 30 + 5

550. 100 + 40 + 7

Page 40:   Place Value: Expanded Notation

551. 759	552. 16	553. 144	554. 603	555. 51	556. 295
557. 758	558. 355	559. 189	560. 248	561. 982	562. 136
563. 528	564. 867	565. 729	566. 718	567. 692	568. 821
569. 785	570. 134	571. 870	572. 542	573. 243	574. 935
575. 930	576. 274	577. 413	578. 762	579. 670	580. 40

581. 449   582. 739   583. 688   584. 385   585. 607   586. 116

587. 813   588. 159   589. 833   590. 427   591. 545   592. 859

593. 130   594. 322   595. 661   596. 639   597. 448   598. 377

599. 93   600. 617   601. 667   602. 879   603. 901   604. 276

605. 218   606. 772   607. 209   608. 672   609. 777   610. 881

611. 995   612. 685   613. 150   614. 799   615. 244   616. 447

617. 143   618. 261   619. 614   620. 904   621. 534   622. 987

623. 359   624. 587   625. 12   626. 779   627. 115   628. 269

629. 634   630. 964   631. 386   632. 577   633. 421   634. 781

635. 786   636. 110   637. 390   638. 343   639. 605   640. 486

641. 58   642. 549   643. 175   644. 613   645. 330   646. 79

647. 216   648. 497   649. 188   650. 761   651. 85   652. 679

653. 522   654. 314   655. 265   656. 438   657. 658   658. 594

659. 404   660. 916   661. 610   662. 109   663. 728   664. 18

665. 659   666. 34   667. 272   668. 300   669. 49   670. 39

671. 836   672. 166   673. 783   674. 535   675. 55   676. 138

677. 624   678. 338   679. 104   680. 473

Page 51: Place Value: Expanded Notation

681. eighty-five   682. ninety-five   683. sixty-nine

684. two   685. nine   686. ninety-one

687. sixty-three   688. ninety-four   689. eight

690. eighty-nine

691. thirty-two

692. seventy

693. fifty-six

694. forty-seven

695. forty-nine

696. five

697. seventy-five

698. seventy-one

699. twenty-eight

700. forty-three

701. eighty-eight

702. seven

703. thirty-six

704. fifteen

705. ninety-nine

706. seventy-two

707. forty

708. ninety-two

709. six

710. nineteen

711. twenty

712. fifty-nine

713. thirty

714. ninety-seven

715. three

716. eleven

717. seventy-seven

718. twenty-nine

719. forty-eight

720. eighty-four

721. fifty

722. sixty-eight

723. fourteen

724. fifty-one

725. thirty-one

726. twenty-one

727. forty-two

728. eighty-one

729. seventy-four

730. sixty-five

731. thirty-seven

732. ninety

733. sixty

734. seventy-three

735. fifty-three

736. eighteen

737. sixty-six

738. forty-one

739. twenty-two

740. thirty-four

741. ten

742. seventy-eight

743. twenty-five

744. twenty-four

745. twelve

746. seventy-nine

747. seventy-six

748. fifty-eight

749. thirty-nine

750. sixteen

751. thirteen

752. twenty-seven

753. sixty-two

754. eighty-three

755. four

756. ninety-three

757. eighty-six

758. thirty-eight

759. fifty-four

760. ninety-six

761. sixty-four

762. one

763. seventeen

764. eighty-two

765. sixty-seven

766. ninety-eight

767. fifty-two

768. forty-six

769. fifty-seven

770. thirty-five

771. sixty-one

772. forty-four

773. fifty-five

774. one hundred